MYSTERIES of the
PHARAOHS

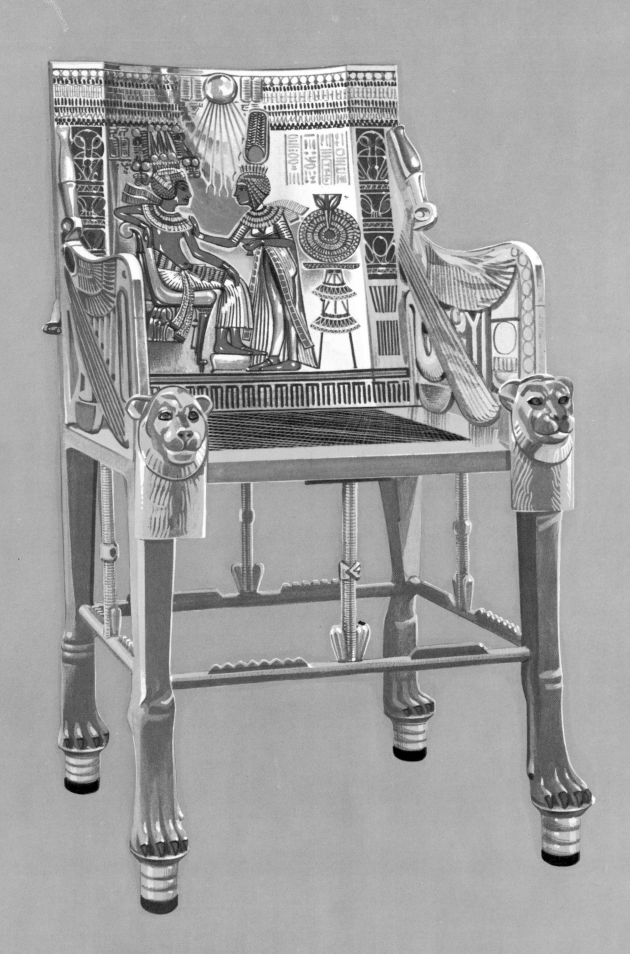

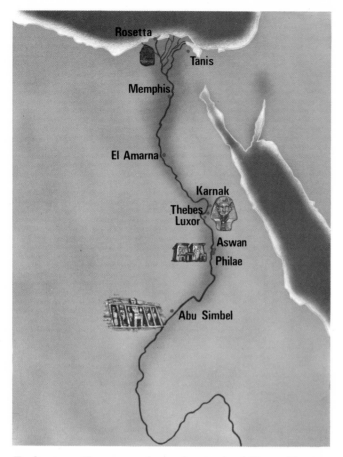

Rosetta
Tanis
Memphis
El Amarna
Karnak
Thebes
Luxor
Aswan
Philae
Abu Simbel

Endpaper: Treasures from the tomb of Tutankhamen: golden throne, pectoral ornament, earring, alabaster vase and model of Anubis, the dog-shaped god.

Photographs by courtesy of Popperfoto (page 7, Carter, page 45, Abu Simbel), the Griffith Institute, Ashmolean Museum (pages 8 and 9, Tutankhamen's tomb, page 12, Carter and Carnarvon), the British Museum (page 17, Rosetta Stone, Jean François Champollion), Radio Times Hulton Picture Library (page 40, Alexander the Great, page 41, Ptolemy, page 42, Napoleon, page 43, Belzoni), Barnaby's Picture Library (page 43, temple of Queen Hatshepsut, and back endpaper, Ramseum) Egyptian State Tourist Administration (page 44, Abu Simbel), and Twentieth Century-Fox (page 41, *Cleopatra* still). *Map: Roland Berry*

Published in the United States by Rand McNally and Company 1977

Designed and produced by Intercontinental Book Productions

Contents

IN SEARCH OF LOST WORLDS

MYSTERIES of the PHARAOHS

Written by Robin May

Illustrated by Christine Molan and Brian Edwards

Rand McNally & Company

Chicago   New York   San Francisco

I   The years of excavation
The opening of a pharaoh's tomb

He had waited so long for this moment, but what lay behind the door? There was every indication that the tomb robbers had been there before him, the thieves who had stripped every other tomb in the fabulous Valley of the Kings of its treasures. Would there be anything worthwhile left in this, the last resting place of the little-known pharaoh Tutankhamen, except for the usual wall paintings and carvings? However fascinating, these could not be as exciting as an unplundered tomb.

It was time to act, rather than think. Howard Carter, soon to be the most famous archaeologist in the world, began to cut a hole in the door in front of him. It had to be big enough for a candle to be passed through.

Behind Carter was his rich patron and helper, Lord Carnarvon, whose daughter, Lady Evelyn Herbert, stood nervously beside him. Carter's devoted assistant, Mr. Callender, was there too. They had suffered many disappointments already, yet nothing could prevent a tense excitement overwhelming them as they watched Carter make the opening in the door's top left corner.

The intense heat of the air released from the room beyond almost blew out the candle which he passed through the hole; then, the flame glowed and the eager archaeologist could see what lay beyond. As he later wrote, "Details of the room emerged slowly from the mist, strange animals, statues, and gold – everywhere the glint of gold."

Lord Carnarvon, unable to stand the strain any longer, demanded: "Can you see anything?"

There was another pause, seemingly endless, then Carter spoke.

"Yes, wonderful things."

This great day was November 26, 1922, and four days later the news broke to a thrilled world. Neither Carter nor anyone else was to realize at first just how colossal the treasure-trove was. His discovery was to prove the greatest, most marvelous and also the most important find in the history of Egyptian archaeology.

It was to take more than seven years to complete work on the tomb of Tutankhamen, by the end of which no less than two thousand objects, many beyond price, would have been found.

However, the saga of the search for the tomb had begun long before the day when Howard Carter saw his "wonderful things."

Because the ancient Egyptians believed that a dead man's spirit lived on in his body, every

Howard Carter clearing the tomb.

effort was made to make that body immortal. Naturally, the pharaoh, the god-king, demanded extra attention, and long before Tutankhamen's reign (which began about 1350 B.C.), the rulers of Egypt had built great pyramids as tombs.

We shall return to these astounding "staircases to heaven," but it should be noted that pyramids had one serious disadvantage: this type of "mansion of eternity" was more than somewhat conspicuous! Thus the tomb robbers – and there were vast numbers of them, eager to get at the treasures within – knew exactly where to look.

The loot included the dead man's most precious and important possessions for his use in the next world. His body, if the man was rich, was skillfully preserved by special spices and salts. This process is known as mummification. When the art was at its peak, about 1200 B.C., the priests who practiced it took up to seventy days to perfect their work, first removing the entrails, which are hard to preserve, and storing them elsewhere.

The pharaohs spent years constructing their tombs. It was not that the ancient Egyptians were morbid – they seem to have been a most stable and contented people – but it was common sense to make the best of the next world as well as the present one.

By Tutankhamen's time, the pharaohs were buried secretly in the Valley of the Kings on the west bank of the Nile opposite their capital, Thebes. In earlier times the capital had been at

The entrance to Tutankhamen's tomb.

Memphis to the north in lower Egypt ("lower" meaning the lower reaches of the Nile), and it was there that the pyramids were built.

The Valley of the Kings lies behind a mountain barrier beyond the fertile strip of the Nile and in the desert. It is hidden away in a fold in the cliffs. Security was total, or so the kings of Egypt hoped. One inscription by the architect Ineni, who built a tomb for an earlier pharaoh, Thutmosis I, reads: "I supervised the excavation of His Majesty's tomb in the hills secretly, with none to see or hear."

But the tomb robbers were too clever for him – in modern as well as ancient times. When Howard Carter made his find, every other tomb in the Valley had been discovered, and all of them had been found robbed, most of them completely. Only the inner chambers of Tutankhamen's tomb were found intact, and their treasures proved incomparable. Yet he was a minor pharaoh. One can hardly begin to imagine what must have been stolen from tombs of far greater rulers.

Fortunately, the walls of these other tombs with their marvelous paintings and limestone frescoes have revealed to the world in picture form just how rich and exciting a life many of the ancient Egyptians lived, and how generally content the mass of the population was.

Yet Tutankhamen, the best known of these ancient Egyptians, was hardly more than a name until discovery by the formidable team of Carter

and Carnarvon ensured his immortality.

Luck played a key role in the trail to the tomb. The immensely rich Lord Carnarvon, born in 1866, was not interested in Egyptology (the study of ancient Egypt) until his doctor advised him to visit Egypt for his health's sake in 1902, after he had been badly injured in a car crash. He liked spending his fortune to some purpose, and digging up the past seemed an ideal use for it.

Meanwhile, Howard Carter, the son of an illustrator, and seven years younger than Carnarvon, had come to Egypt in 1892, originally as a draftsman. But drawing Egyptian relics and plans of tombs was not enough for him and he soon began excavating. The word spread that a brilliant young scholar was at work and in 1907 he was introduced to the man with whom he would eventually share worldwide fame.

The pair found plenty of relics between 1908 and 1912 (even now something of interest is found almost daily), but nothing sensational. At the same time a rich American, Theodore Davis, was doing remarkable work in the Valley of the Kings. By 1909 he had decided: "I fear that the Valley of the Tombs [the Valley of the Kings] is now exhausted." In fact, he thought that one of his discoveries, a small pit tomb, must be the tomb of Tutankhamen. It contained nothing but an alabaster figure and a wooden box with pieces of gold foil, on which were the names of the king and his wife, Queen Ankhesnamun.

He also found something far more important, though he did not realize its significance – jars with broken pottery used at the funeral feasts, fragments of linen with the king's name on them, and other material used for mummification.

Carter realized what the find meant. It proved to him that the tomb of the king was in the Valley, still waiting to be found.

He made a big map of the area and, with infinite patience, searched almost every part of it with Carnarvon. The First World War (1914–18) held up progress, but finally there was nothing left to examine but a small triangle of ground in front of the enormous tomb of Ramses VI. This area had been left till last because to dig it up would prevent visitors reaching the tomb of the great pharaoh.

By now even Carnarvon was getting discouraged. Over 200,000 tons of rubble and sand had been moved during the search, to no avail. In the summer of 1922 he had had enough.

The Valley of the Kings. The tomb of Tutankhamen lies under the entrance to the tomb of Ramses VI, above center. In the background towers the Theban peak.

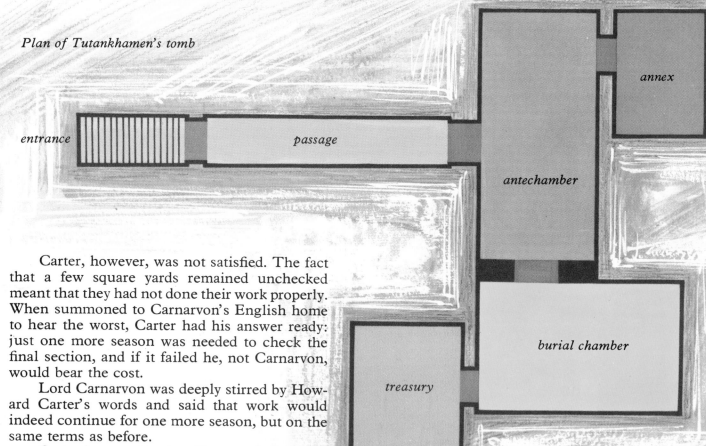

Plan of Tutankhamen's tomb

entrance

passage

annex

antechamber

burial chamber

treasury

Carter, however, was not satisfied. The fact that a few square yards remained unchecked meant that they had not done their work properly. When summoned to Carnarvon's English home to hear the worst, Carter had his answer ready: just one more season was needed to check the final section, and if it failed he, not Carnarvon, would bear the cost.

Lord Carnarvon was deeply stirred by Howard Carter's words and said that work would indeed continue for one more season, but on the same terms as before.

Carter hastened back to Egypt and was ready to start work on November 1, 1922, just in front of the entrance to Ramses VI's tomb. First he uncovered huts used by the ancient workmen, though some of these he had found five years before. Then, on November 4, having removed the first hut completely, he came upon a step cut into the rock floor. A day later twelve steps had been cleared.

In front of him and his hand-picked, trustworthy workers was the upper part of a doorway which had been blocked up and plastered over and which bore a royal seal. Excitement coupled with the fear of disappointment must have governed his emotions in those anxious days, for it was only too probable that the end of it all would be yet another empty, plundered tomb.

With Callender's help, Carter cleared the last four steps and found the lower part of the doorway, also plastered over and also bearing royal seals. They had reached the final barrier, and there upon it was the seal of Tutankhamen. But did it mean that they had found the tomb?

Certainly it was worth summoning Lord Carnarvon, and a cable was sent: "At last have made wonderful discovery in the Valley; a magnificent tomb with seals intact; recovered same for your arrival; congratulations."

By "recovering" Carter meant filling in the passage to prevent unwanted intruders. Then, leaving trusted workmen on guard, he sent his telegram, and settled down, not without apprehension, to wait.

Lord Carnarvon and his daughter reached Luxor, the modern town beside Thebes, on November 23. The next day the whole staircase was cleared. Carter's spirits sank when it became clear that the door before him showed signs of having been opened, then closed again; but perhaps not much had been taken by robbers, he reasoned, or officials would not have bothered to reseal the tomb.

The stone blocks were removed and beyond it he saw a tunnel filled with rubble, and about eleven yards (ten meters) along it a second door, also sealed by the necropolis (cemetery) officials and bearing the seal of Tutankhamen.

For Carter that November day was "the day of days, the most wonderful that I have ever lived through, and certainly one whose like I can never hope to see again."

The room he had looked into was the antechamber, itself a true Ali Baba's cave. It took several months for the antechamber to be cleared, for the robbers had not managed to make the most of their forced entry. Besides, everything had to be

10

*Below: guardian statue.
Left: the jumble of
objects found in the
antechamber.*

handled with the utmost care, recorded, photographed, guarded, and transported – finally to the Cairo Museum. By February 17, 1923, there were only two life-size wooden statues of Tutankhamen left in the room, guarding another door.

On the day that this was due to be opened, the onlookers included experts from Britain, America, and Egypt. Beyond, the world waited, for the tomb of Tutankhamen had been headline news ever since the story broke. Indeed, so popular was the story that Carter and his men had experienced great difficulty in continuing with their work owing to the flood of visitors which had been attracted to the scene.

Carter, his hands trembling, began chipping away at the door to the burial chamber and did not stop until he had made a hole big enough for a torch to be inserted.

He had seen treasures enough in the antechamber, but what he saw now took his breath away. There before him was a wall of gold!

The stone blocks which filled the doorway were difficult to remove, even with eager helpers, for they were very heavy and of uneven size. But after two hours the task was completed.

A hush fell over the onlookers. In front of them was a sight no modern man had ever seen – the intact funeral chamber of a pharaoh. He had been a minor monarch who had died in his late teens. His reign had been brief, yet this stupendous display was in his honor.

The tomb's treasures

No one knows what the tomb of a *major* pharaoh was like, for few of us can imagine anything more splendid than Tutankhamen's.

The royal body lay magnificently protected by four shrines of gilded wood, one inside the other. They enclosed a mighty sarcophagus (coffin) of quartzite, which in turn housed three coffins, one of them made of solid gold.

In the innermost coffin was the mummy of the young king, dressed in royal trappings. On his head was a breathtaking gold mask, modeled to the king's features, and on his body were jewels and magic charms.

The treasury beyond the burial chamber contained such riches as a golden wooden shrine holding the mummified remains of the king's internal organs and an effigy of the dog-shaped Anubis, god of the dead, guardian of the necropolis and master of mummification. A small annex contained yet more treasures.

On a lotus cup seen by Carter and Carnarvon when they first entered the tomb was the inscription: "May the Ka [immortal spirit] live! Mayest thou spend millions of years, O thou who lovest Thebes, seated with thy face turned to the north

wind and thine eyes contemplating felicity."

Thanks to the two Britons Tutankhamen's name will survive as long as civilization itself. Yet though the discovery of his tomb taught the world so much about ancient Egypt, and though it brought to light so many items intended for his use in the next world – his sandals, fan, and so on – many mysteries about Tutankhamen remain. Experts argue about what facts we do have.

Tutankhamen's predecessor was pharaoh Amenhotep IV. He had resented the all-powerful priesthood of Amon, the sun-god, who ministered to a remarkable number of gods. Amenhotep and his wife, Queen Nefertiti, began to worship the Aten, the sun disk that represented the power of the sun. They left Thebes to set up a new capital at Tell el-Amarna.

The new religion was a joyous, liberty-loving one with a single god, and was far ahead of its time. Though we do not know for sure who Tutankhamen's parents were, he was certainly raised in this new faith. He was first called Tutankhaten (for Aten), then got his later name (for Amon). Many believe that, being only eleven when he came to the throne, he was unable to stand up to the priests. He was forced to make Thebes the capital again, and the old religion flourished. He was only eighteen when he died.

We do not know why he died, or why two stillborn children – presumably his – were buried with him. Nor do we know what happened to his beautiful wife Ankhesnamun. But it seems that Ay, his vizier (prime minister), ruled for a time after him as Tutankhamen had no living children.

Later, the angry priests tried to remove all memories of Ay, Akhenaten (the name Amenhotep IV had taken), Tutankhamen and the rival capital city, along with the revolutionary religion. Thanks to Carter and Carnarvon, they failed. One inscription found reads, "To speak the name of the dead is to make them live again [for it restores] the breath of life." This is just what has happened. Tutankhamen's tomb is one of Egypt's greatest tourist attractions. The tomb's fabulous treasures are now in the Cairo Museum, except on the rare occasions when they are allowed to leave Egypt for exhibitions abroad.

The Tutankhamen discovery gave rise to a legend too . . . the mystery of the mummy's curse. The story of the curse begins with a tragic event, the death of Lord Carnarvon. He was bitten by a mosquito at Luxor, which developed into a blood infection and then pneumonia. On April 5, 1923, a mere month after the tomb itself was discovered, he died in Cairo. However, he had at least lived to see those "wonderful things."

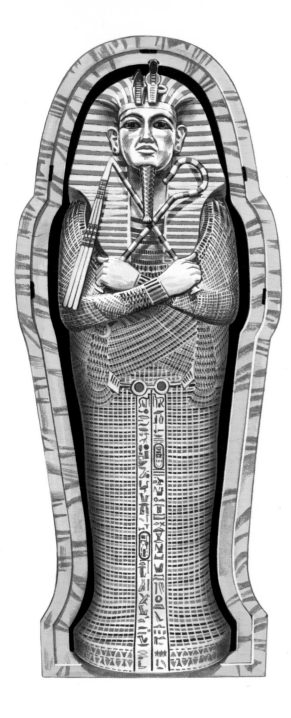

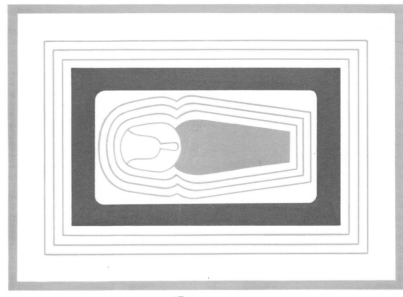

Above is one of the four "mummiform" coffins of Tutankhamen, while on the right is his magnificent gold mask, the finest funerary mask ever found. Above right is a diagram showing how the four golden shrines and the three mummiform coffins fitted tightly into each other.

Opposite page: Carter (right) and Carnarvon opening the door to the burial chamber.

"The Curse of the pharaoh"

The straightforward reason for Lord Carnarvon's death did not satisfy many easily fooled members of the public. Surely Tutankhamen had struck the noble lord down for daring to open his tomb! Were there not inscriptions (obviously intended for tomb robbers) making dire threats against the living who "come to violate the tombs?" "The Curse of the Pharaoh," in the words of one newspaper, had clearly done its worst. Or perhaps Carnarvon had touched some poisoned object left by the original guardians of the tombs.

Then the head of the Department of Egyptian Antiquities at the Louvre Museum in Paris, Georges Bénédite, died from a stroke, doubtless brought on by the ovenlike heat of the Valley. Next Arthur Mace, an official of New York's Metropolitan Museum of Art, died. The curse had now struck thrice!

Eager reporters managed to work the final death toll up to twenty-one, though many of the people concerned had little to do with the find.

The entire curse theory can be shown to be a total fraud by the merest glance at those who survived its fatal impact. Among them is the one person upon whom the pharaoh would clearly have wrought vengeance first, Howard Carter. He lived on until 1939, many years after his find, and died at the age of sixty-six. As for Dr. Derry, the expert who performed the crucial anatomical examination of the mummy of the dead king, he died long after in his eighties. Many others immediately concerned with the tomb-opening and early examinations also lived to ripe old ages. Yet even in the 1970s some newspapers have begun to bring out the old fables once again.

And yet . . . there were two strange occurrences, both of which date from the time that Lord Carnarvon died.

The first happened in Cairo at 1:55 a.m. on April 5, 1923, at the very moment of his death. Not only did every electric light in his hotel go out, but so did every light in the whole of Cairo. The engineer in charge of the city's lighting could never offer an explanation of why it happened.

And at that very moment in far-off England, Lord Carnarvon's dog uttered a terrible series of howls – and died.

Those who believe in the nonsensical curse theory may feel that these two events prove their case. If we are to be fanciful, however, surely it is

Tutankhamen pictured on the back of his gold-plated throne.

possible to assume that the lights were dimmed by Tutankhamen as a tribute to one of the men who had restored him to fame? And the dog? His mournful tribute, whether accidental or by design, is unlikely to relate to a curse, though by any standards it is a good story, and a true one, verified by Carnarvon's son, Lord Porchester.

The public, fascinated by the curse theory, would not – and in some cases will not – accept that it had been fooled. Naturally, filmmakers have eagerly exploited such gullibility. The film industry was booming in the 1920s, but it was not until 1932, when the "talkies" had finally ousted the silent films, that *The Mummy* was made. It starred the celebrated horror-film actor Boris Karloff, in private life a quiet Englishman who liked cricket. In this film he played a very vigorous 3000-year-old mummy who came back to life to look for his long-lost love.

There was a lull after this popular but rather silly epic, but things started booming again in the 1940s with *The Mummy's Hand*, *The Mummy's Tomb*, *The Mummy's Ghost*, and *The Mummy's Curse*. In the late 1950s and early 1960s Hammer Films also entered the mummy business, beginning with a re-make of *The Mummy* starring Christopher Lee. There have been mummy comedies, too, including *Mummy's Boys*, the Three Stooges in *Mummy's Dummies*, and *Abbott and Costello Meet the Mummy*.

Strangely, Tutankhamen himself had been cursed after death by Ay's successor, King Horemheb, who was determined to wipe out every vestige of the Atenite heresy. This was the new religion that, as we have seen, was preached by the young king's predecessor, Amenhotep IV, who became Akhenaten. Horemheb actually had Tutankhamen erased from the official list of pharaohs. It is very fortunate that he did not also decide to seize the king's funerary treasures.

Now the name of Horemheb is forgotten except by experts in Egyptology, and the curse he put on Tutankhamen is not simply lifted but totally forgotten, thanks to Howard Carter and Lord Carnarvon. The supporters of the mighty Amon, or Amon himself, might be thought by the fanciful to have been responsible for the curse, even though their first victim would undoubtedly have been Carter. But happily the attempts of Amon and his followers to make Carter vanish forever were futile.

Among the treasures of Tutankhamen were the pendant, scarab bracelet and pectoral (ornamental breastplate) shown above. The pendant shows the vulture-goddess of the South, Nekhabet. The scarab beetle featured on the other two items was considered sacred.

The key to Egypt's past

The biggest breakthrough in the entire history of Egyptology was the finding of the Rosetta Stone. Pierre Bouchard, an engineer officer in Napoleon's army, came across it in 1799 half buried in mud near Rosetta on the Nile delta, and it was later taken to the British Museum.

On the stone was a decree written by priests of Ptolemy V in three languages. The first was in hieroglyphics, totally unintelligible in 1799, the second in demotic, the popular language in Ptolemy's day (c. 200 B.C.), and the third in ancient Greek, which was understood by many scholars. One of them, Jean Francois Champollion (1790–1832), was an expert on eastern languages and it was chiefly through his efforts that the secret of the hieroglyphics and of demotic was worked out, the Greek providing an essential guide. From the 1820s, Egyptian writing was a mystery no longer.

The study of ancient Egypt blossomed, though at first not very scientifically. Prominent in the early period was Giovanni Belzoni (1778–1823), a former circus "strong man," just under six feet (two meters) tall, who had studied engineering in his spare time. This Italian became very popular in theatrical London before going to Egypt, where he transported the colossal bust of Ramses II first from Thebes to Alexandria by river, then by sea to London. His huge work force got the bust – now in the British Museum – to the Nile using a carrier pulled by ropes, and placing an endless row of poles in front of the carrier for it to roll over.

Later, Belzoni started excavations, using methods that have astounded modern archaeologists. He even resorted to a battering ram to unearth treasures. Belzoni was a true pioneer, though Sir Flinders Petrie (1853–1942) was the first archaeologist to work on scientific principles, and the most renowned of all Egyptologists. Today, despite many gaps in our knowledge, we know enough about ancient Egypt to marvel at its civilization.

Ancient Egypt and the great river Nile were virtually one and the same. To the north, the people were protected by the Mediterranean, while along the river's banks was a rich fertile strip, beyond which lay desert. For more than a hundred days every year the Nile spilled over the fields of the strip. It left behind rich black soil, most of it carried down from the Blue Nile, which began its life high in the uplands of Ethiopia, joining the White Nile at what is now Khartoum.

Egypt became a single nation about 3200

B.C. when King Menes of upper Egypt conquered lower Egypt and united the two, making Memphis his capital. It was about this time that the people learned to irrigate and use the plow.

When the third dynasty (family) of rulers came to power, it marked the beginning of the Old Kingdom (c. 2700–2200 B.C.). During this time of peace the pyramids were built. The biggest was the Great Pyramid of King Cheops, the most stupendous monument constructed by human hands. Built of granite and limestone, it was comprised of some 2,300,000 stone blocks. The original height was 479 feet (146 meters) and the sides of each base were 751 feet (229 meters). Some 100,000 men working in three-month shifts took twenty years to build it, probably when their lands were flooded annually, for they were almost certainly not the downtrodden slaves of legend.

From 2200 to 2050 B.C. there was chaos and civil war, but in the Middle Kingdom (2050–1800 B.C.) Egypt was reunited by Theban nobles and expanded south into Nubia and east as far as Syria. From 1800 to 1570 B.C. chaos reigned again: much of the delta was captured by rovers named Hyksos, equipped with horses, chariots, body armor and new bronze weapons.

There followed the New Kingdom (c. 1570–1085 B.C.) when the invaders were driven out, mighty monuments were built and trade with other parts of Africa began. Under Thutmose III, Egypt's empire was extended to the Euphrates in Asia and south to below the fourth cataract of the Nile, and Thebes became the capital of the known world.

Jean François Champollion

The Rosetta Stone

The Sphinx, an immense figure 256 feet long and 35 feet high, was sculpted from a huge mass of rock left behind in a quarry as unsuitable for building purposes. It has the body of a lion and the head of a king. It stands guard before the Second Pyramid.

II Nekhebu's story
The great lord's estate

Now let us go back in time to the reign of Ramses II, known as Ramses the Great, who ruled from about 1292 to 1225 B.C., and meet a boy, not yet nine years old, called Nekhebu. Tutankhamen had been dead for more than half a century, but the boy's homeland was much the same as it had been for a thousand years before.

Nekhebu was the son of a landholder who worked as an overseer on a great lord's estate. The fact that he had land of his own was not unusual, for even humble peasants had some land, though they were bound to the masters. But they were not slaves. They could own cattle and donkeys and, if they prospered, could buy decent linen for their wives to wear. Some of the better off even had furniture in their small, flat-roofed, white-painted houses of dried mud or bricks: in Nekhebu's house were a bed and chairs, for instance.

Each year had three seasons. The first was when the Nile flooded and reached its height, the second when the waters fell. As the waters retreated, the peasants would scatter the seed. Two cows would drag the wooden plows and, later, sheep and pigs were driven over the fields to make sure the seed was trampled into the soggy ground. Finally the peasants would rake the fields.

The third season, a time of rejoicing, saw the riches of the harvest gathered in.

Farmers grew wheat, barley, flax, cucumbers, leeks, and beans, and kept ducks, geese, and goats as well as sheep and cows. Donkeys and oxen did much of the heavier agricultural work.

Most of the peasants enjoyed life except on the rare occasions when the harvest was poor, and most of the landowners were good masters. Even the local magistrates were often quite lenient with wrongdoers. The ancient Egyptian rulers were rarely tyrants, and it was only in certain times of civil strife that the peasants' lives were ever unhappy.

There was plenty to be done all the year round. Not only did the crops have to be sown and reaped, cattle bred, and bees tended, among countless other farming jobs, but every year the workers had to lay down tools and help in government works for a time – anything from repairing dikes and roads to digging new canals. A number of festivals took place throughout the year, too, especially at harvest time. A special field was reserved for the peasants of each estate to gather as much corn as they could reap in a single day.

The harvested grain was stored in granaries, where scribes (men who could write) kept records of the amounts of grain brought in.

Young Nekhebu was fascinated by these men and longed to read and write. It was not that the prospect of hard work in the fields depressed him, but he liked the idea of the life of a scribe. So did his parents, but they could not imagine any way in which their son could leap from peasant boy to educated government employee. He would normally have spent his life as his parents had, rising to become an overseer like his father. However, the lad's eagerness to get on in life had been noted by the estate-owner; his officials reported how bright young Nekhebu was. The nobleman decided to help Nekhebu.

Such favors were unusual in ancient Egypt, where classes tended to be rigidly divided; Nekhebu's parents were surprised and delighted that the great lord was giving their son this chance.

To become a scribe, young Nekhebu would have to go to a school for scribes, in Thebes, almost 100 miles (160 km) up the river. There was sadness in the family, for they were very close. They enjoyed a happy, contented family life in which the women played an important part. Women were not educated, whatever their class. Nekhebu's father was thrilled, for he knew that many opportunities would be open to his son: a royal servant, a lawyer or a diplomat, an engineer or an architect. The world would be at his feet.

Journey up the Nile

Father and son started up the Nile toward Thebes. The mighty river was Egypt's main road as well as its lifeblood, and the pair had a considerable way to travel in their small boat made of papyrus reeds lashed together with poles.

For some way they rowed alongside another papyrus boat, whose owner had come all the way from the lush marshlands of the delta, where the Nile broke up into innumerable channels large and small and flowed out into the Mediterranean.

Naturally, the bigger boats on the busy river were made of wood, though there was a great shortage of timber in Egypt. By the time of Ramses II's reign most wood was being imported.

There were single-sail boats to be seen and

Nekhebu and his father journey to Thebes in a humble papyrus craft. Among the river traffic they see are merchant boats and the very elaborate royal craft of cedarwood shown here on the right. Its underside is brightly painted and decorated with gold leaf.

some dug-out canoes, and once on the journey they saw a splendid galley with a double bank of oars. Finest of all was a smaller boat with a handsome-looking cabin amidships which, they decided, must have belonged to some very high-ranking official. The two steering oars were bigger than any they had ever seen.

As well as boats, the Nile teemed with enormous rafts, the number of which increased as the pair neared Thebes. They needed to be big and strong, for they carried huge blocks of stone from quarries to the cities for the construction of giant statues and temples. Similar rafts had been used to transport pyramid blocks centuries before.

On one occasion a strange-looking boat, very high at the bows and the stern and with a cabin in the middle, passed by. It was being towed by another vessel with a single sail, but powered mainly by oarsmen. When Nekhebu asked his father the purpose of the strange boat, in which he could see animals at one end but a crew of only two people manning the twin rudders at the stern, his father said that the people were making a religious pilgrimage. The animals were for food.

Now they were approaching Thebes. The river banks seemed to be lined with a succession of temples, among which, on the west bank, stood the magnificent temple of Queen Hatshepsut at Deir el-Bahri. Now they could see Thebes itself, the most splendid city of the day, where young Nekhebu was to live with his aunt and attend school in one of the temples.

Arrival in the capital

As they drew closer, Nekhebu rejoiced in the bustle and noise and color of the scene. He had never left his home before, nor had he ever seen such vast numbers of people, thronging the shore and bustling about the river in every sort of boat. They had arrived in Thebes!

This great city was the capital of Egypt for much of the reign of Ramses II. Later, because of constant wars in Syria and Palestine, Ramses II was to make Tanis in the delta his headquarters. By then, long after Nekhebu's school days there, the king would have consolidated the work of earlier pharaohs and made Thebes a breathtaking sight.

Ramses II planned on a large scale, and under him Egypt reached new magnificence. He had seized the throne from his brother some years before Nekhebu reached Thebes and been crowned with awe-inspiring ceremony. During his reign, the Egyptian empire would be extended from distant Syria to near the Nile's fourth cataract far to the south.

This empire building and maintenance involved a much larger army than was usual for the Egyptians: they were not a war-loving people,

In Thebes, Nekhebu witnesses a procession of priests and temple bearers headed by the great Ramses on a day of religious festivity.

but under Ramses II the army was 20,000 strong. His most famous battles were frequently described on the monuments commissioned by the pharaoh.

Ramses II also put a great deal of his energies into building. He built monuments all over the country, including the stupendous rock temple at Abu Simbel, the temple at Luxor near Thebes, the Ramseum – his mortuary temple at Thebes – and the temple at Karnak, the city's crowning glory, which he completed.

When Nekhebu and his father arrived in Thebes, they first spent some time seeing the city. They gazed in amazement at two triumphs of an earlier pharaoh, Amenhotep III: the Malkata Palace and the Colossi of Memnon. These last were monumental statues in front of his temple, which was given its modern name by later Greek travelers, who called Amenhotep "Memnon" after one of their gods.

Nekhebu and his father looked at the Ramseum, still in its early stages of construction, and visited the temple of Luxor, one of the finest groups of buildings in the whole fabulous kingdom. Then it was time to visit Karnak, which is regarded by many today as the most marvelous of all the religious shrines of ancient Egypt.

Father and son walked along the avenue linking Luxor and Karnak, a long, wide road with ram-headed sphinxes on either side. The great Amenhotep used this royal highroad, almost a mile (1.5 kilometers) long, for processions. The excited pair saw a temple pylon ahead of them, the first of ten at Karnak. Each pylon consisted of massive twin towers, in the shape of flattened pyramids, connected by an impressive gateway.

At last they came to Karnak itself, the shrine of Amon-Re, the king of the gods. Almost a city in itself, Karnak was crowded with people, including a great many stonemasons, hard at work. Among other marvels was the lofty pylon of Amenhotep III, who had torn down a building of a previous pharaoh to help build it.

Egyptian kings did not hesitate to use the monuments of earlier rulers as building materials. Sometimes they even chiseled out inscriptions on earlier buildings and substituted their own names!

What impressed young Nekhebu most was the Hypostyle Hall. The word "hypostyle" means "a roof supported by pillars," and that is exactly what this magnificent building was. It had recently been completed by Ramses after having been started by his predecessor, Seti I.

Standing in a vast court, it was 334.6 feet (102 meters) wide and 190.3 feet (58 meters) long. Both

Nekhebu visits the Hypostyle Hall at Karnak, the temple of Amon. Its columns, nearly 10 feet in diameter, are decorated with ceremonial scenes which make a vivid impression on the young boy.

the thick inner columns and the thinner outer ones, 78.7 feet (24 meters) high, were decorated with paintings. To this day, the Hypostyle Hall remains the largest columned hall ever built. Young Nekhebu felt a sudden chill of cold and excitement when he entered the hall from the blazing courtyard outside. He had never seen, or even imagined, such splendor. All too soon, however, he would have to leave this wonderful place and go to the home of his aunt, for tomorrow his school days would begin.

School for Nekhebu

Apart from the beatings, Nekhebu found school even more enjoyable than he had dared hope it would be. None of the boys escaped the rod, for discipline was tough in the cool temple classroom. The priest teachers had a maxim: "A boy's ear is on his back," though this has been translated as "in his backside!"

Nearly all the pupils were day boys. Nekhebu set out from his aunt's house every morning with a small basket containing bread and a jug of beer. He usually fell in with some of his fellow pupils on the way. They reached the temple full of high spirits, but once work began, under the teacher's watchful eye, they soon calmed down.

Reading and writing were the first lessons. Pupils did not use papyrus (paper made from reeds) to write on for some time, because until they became skilled it was considered wasteful. Instead, they wrote on polished limestone blocks that had lines or squares marked on them. Later,

each pupil would be issued his own roll of papyrus on which he could write, using his reed pens and red and black inks. He had to master some seven hundred characters.

There were three styles of writing to be learned. First there were hieroglyphics (meaning "sacred carvings" in ancient Greek), a mixture of signs and pictures that the Egyptians had always used on their monuments and for their formal inscriptions. Hieroglyphics, used in Egypt since about 3000 B.C., were magnificent to look at but hard to write fast. So hieratic (from a Greek word for "priestly") was introduced. This was really a shorthand version of hieroglyphics, and by Nekhebu's time official documents were written in hieratic.

Finally, demotic was invented, which could be written even faster. It means "popular" in Greek. Readers will recall that the Rosetta Stone was written in hieroglyphics, demotic, and Greek.

Nekhebu was also taught to be a draftsman and painter, using blue, green, yellow, and white inks to illuminate his writings. Scribes could progress to work in a wide range of fields in the course of a lifetime, so it was important that their studies should cover a broad spectrum. Nekhebu learned not simply grammar and arithmetic, but also history, geography, law, administration, and technical and military facts. By the time he was in his mid-teens and nearing the end of his school days, he was used to answering questions such as "How would you organize a military expedition to Syria?", "How many men would you need to transport a statue of such and such a weight?", and could be expected to write a detailed essay on the geography of neighboring countries such as Palestine or Nubia.

The schoolmasters continually reminded their pupils of the advantages of being a scribe. A scribe did no manual work; he had the chance to advance to a high position, even to become the right-hand man of the great pharaoh himself.

It was not all work, and as a change from mathematics and history, there was plenty of sport to be enjoyed. Nekhebu and his friends played ball and leap-frog, running and jumping games, and learned to wrestle. Since horses had been introduced into Egypt during the New Kingdom, many boys also learned to ride or drive chariots. Archery, too, was a popular sport, while the dry heat typical of the Egyptian climate helped encourage athletic activity. Naturally, any boy of spirit wanted to go hunting in the desert, or in the marshes, where those with the necessary skill would hunt birds with boomerangs. Spearing fish was almost as hard and just as exciting, while those youths who had joined the army learned war dances. The schoolmasters did not approve of the army and urged their pupils not to join it, but inevitably, many longed to do so.

Meanwhile the schooling went on day by day. Lessons began early, before it became too hot, and finished at noon, which gave the children plenty of time to enjoy themselves. Beating was not the only punishment though it was the most usual one. Sometimes boys were given the Egyptian equivalent of "lines" to write out.

The children of the pharaoh and his great noblemen had private tutors, though in some cases a royal school was established for them all. Character building was considered important at all levels. Young men were warned not to spend

Hunting wild birds in the marshes with a boomerang.

too much time dancing, or visiting the town's taverns, were expected to stand up when their elders appeared, and were told to love and cherish their mothers, who had done so much for them. God would be angry if they did not do this. "Manners will make people love you," ran one maxim. Even princes were not expected to be idle and were sent into some profession to keep them occupied once their schooling was over.

So Nekhebu's education continued for several years, until the time came when he had to decide what he wanted to do. He could have chosen to become a priest, which was considered the highest form of education, but he had other ideas: in fact, he had so many that his career was to take many different turnings in the years to come.

Nekhebu's career

Perhaps it was the power that reading and writing gave the scribes of ancient Egypt which made them a little too proud. Many of them looked down on the men who quarried the stone and even the craftsmen who sculptured it and wrote hieroglyphics on it, yet what would the great temples, statues and pyramids have been without them?

Young Nekhebu, who became a building supervisor when he left school, made no such mistake, perhaps because he was humbly born, and perhaps because he admired the workers. It required great skill to quarry limestone or other stone with soft copper chisels, to cut into the rock at exactly the right spot, put in wooden wedges, wet them, and let the sun expand them and break the rock. Sometimes the sculptors would make the statues on the spot to save transporting huge blocks. Sometimes they worked in their workshops, where other craftsmen also operated – the artist who cut the hieroglyphs, the metal worker who added such details as the eyes, and the painter. Paint was added for realistic effect, for it was vital to make the statue a true portrait of the great man or woman in question. The statue might eventually be placed in a tomb, after all, so the standard was high and the craftsmen well paid for their pains.

The day on which a finished statue was transported to its destination – tomb, temple, or palace – was often a time of rejoicing. Vast crowds would line the streets to watch the impressive monument go by, and there would be feasting on a sumptuous scale.

Nekhebu's education was tested to the full when he entered his profession. Sometimes he was needed for engineering advice: he might be asked to advise how many men would be needed to transport something, for instance. Sometimes he was in charge of checking that hieroglyphs were inscribed on a sculpture perfectly, marking them in with ink before the specialist began carving them out of the stone. Sometimes he was the chief secretary working on a particular project. Sometimes he would be sent off to supervise tomb painting, ensuring that, in accordance with tradition, the important men were depicted noticeably larger than other people. Among other conventions usually followed was that of showing faces in profile, while bodies were usually portrayed with both shoulders facing the observer. Tomb paintings showed all a man's possessions; he would need them in the next world.

Ramses II was as devoted as any pharaoh in history to the building of monuments, and young Nekhebu became used to seeing him inspecting the work. Gradually, the scribe's quickness and efficiency were recognized and his advice was sought by senior officials of the royal court. Once he took part in a huge expedition to collect a black stone called *bakhen* which looked magnificent when polished, and as a result found himself transferred to the list of army scribes. Despite what his schoolmasters had said about avoiding the army, the life had always appealed to Nekhebu, and, though his duties on the expedition had been engineering rather than military, he had taken the opportunity to learn how to manage a chariot.

When the charioteers discovered that Nekhebu was not haughty with them, like so many of his kind, they showed him the tricks of their exciting occupation. First he mastered the smaller single-horse chariot, then the two-horse war chariot. This was a light two-wheeler made of wickerwork, designed to carry a driver and a fighting man. This warrior would have a shield to protect both men, and was usually armed with a

javelin, a sword, and a bow and arrow. The Egyptians rarely rode astride horses and therefore had no cavalry, but they did use chariots for hunting, and for thrilling races as well. These races became Nekhebu's greatest passion, and he soon developed considerable skill.

On active service

Nekhebu's prowess as a charioteer was soon recognized – finally by the great Ramses II himself, who took Nekhebu on to his military staff as a senior scribe.

Then news came of a war against a desert tribe, the Hittites, which had been harrying the borders of the kingdom for some time. It was Nekhebu's chance to shine in a new role.

He was thrilled by the prospect of seeing action, even though his duties did not officially include fighting. The charioteers were eager to show their skill and courage to their king, and the royal bodyguard, who received extra rations of corn and beef and wine, were anxious to show that they had not become weakened by soft living.

Nekhebu noted with excitement the various armed divisions: archers, spearmen, axmen, and chariotry. To be with the royal bodyguard was a great privilege for him. In normal circumstances, he would have been attached to the supply column, where there was plenty of work for a scribe to do. The trumpets blared and an infantry regiment led the advance into the desert.

During the advance, the only person not on foot seemed to be the great pharaoh, who was

driving his own chariot. The rest marched, for the horses had to be spared as much as possible if they were to be fit for battle in desert conditions. The army carried with it all the supplies it would need, for its destination was a great distance away from the lush Nile Valley.

The Egyptians met the enemy on a vast and empty plain. Both sides drew up their armies without interfering with each other. Except when a surprise attack was planned, or an enemy was holding a strong defensive position, it was usual to prepare for battle formally, with both sides awaiting each other's convenience.

Suddenly, Nekhebu received an order to report to the pharaoh. The king's driver, who was to ride with the pharaoh into battle, had fallen ill, and Nekhebu was to take his place. His heart leaped at the honor.

Nekhebu had confidence in his driving ability, which was what mattered. He knew that his sovereign was a mighty warrior, quite capable of taking over the reins if his driver were killed.

The next day the trumpets blared out once again and the battle commenced. For a while the king left the fighting to his commanders, but when, after a time, he noticed that his right flank showed signs of weakening, he and his bodyguard headed toward it to see what they could do. The enemy had cut part of an infantry regiment to pieces when suddenly Ramses and his chariots tore down at them.

Nekhebu was too concerned with controlling the chariot to have time to be frightened, but he saw an archer raise his bow at the pharaoh.

The pharaoh had seen it, too, and as Nekhebu steadied the chariot, the great monarch hurled his javelin and transfixed the archer. Then the horses plunged them back into the thick of the fighting again.

All around were splendidly decorated chariots in broken heaps, the bodies of friend and foe lying strewn on the plain, war cries ringing out, and great clouds of arrows piercing the skies. Then, suddenly, it was over. The enemy had succumbed to the power of the pharaoh and fled back to their native hills. It would be some time before the Hittites dared to challenge the mighty pharaoh of Egypt again.

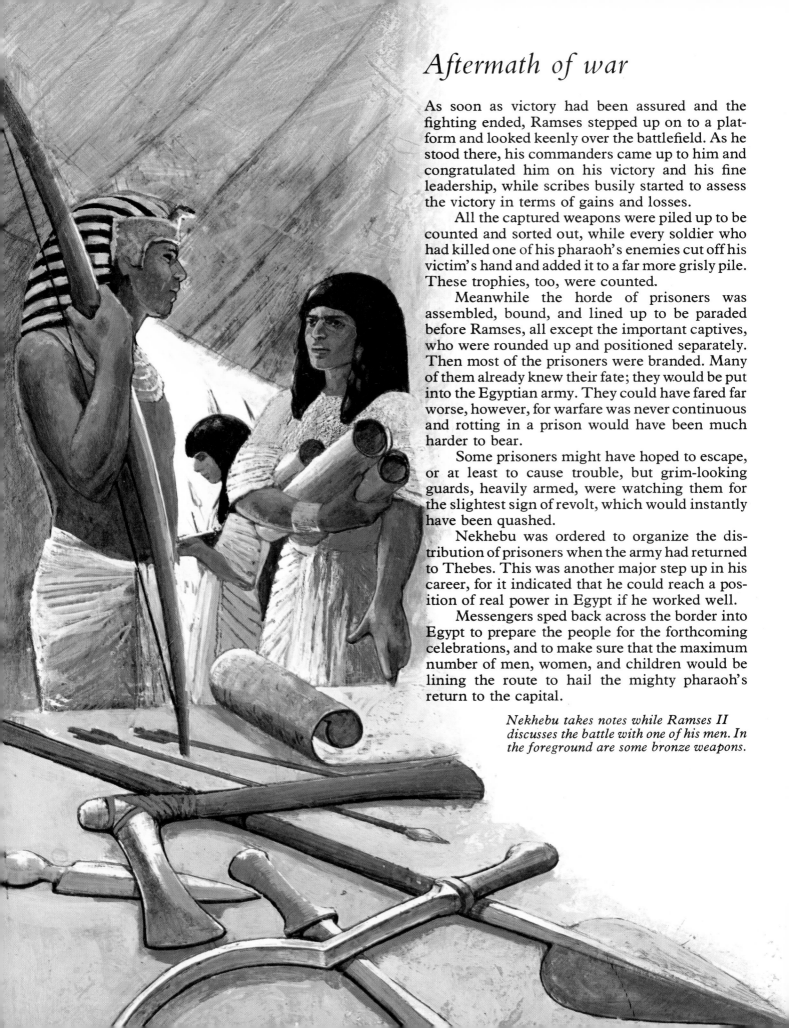

Aftermath of war

As soon as victory had been assured and the fighting ended, Ramses stepped up on to a platform and looked keenly over the battlefield. As he stood there, his commanders came up to him and congratulated him on his victory and his fine leadership, while scribes busily started to assess the victory in terms of gains and losses.

All the captured weapons were piled up to be counted and sorted out, while every soldier who had killed one of his pharaoh's enemies cut off his victim's hand and added it to a far more grisly pile. These trophies, too, were counted.

Meanwhile the horde of prisoners was assembled, bound, and lined up to be paraded before Ramses, all except the important captives, who were rounded up and positioned separately. Then most of the prisoners were branded. Many of them already knew their fate; they would be put into the Egyptian army. They could have fared far worse, however, for warfare was never continuous and rotting in a prison would have been much harder to bear.

Some prisoners might have hoped to escape, or at least to cause trouble, but grim-looking guards, heavily armed, were watching them for the slightest sign of revolt, which would instantly have been quashed.

Nekhebu was ordered to organize the distribution of prisoners when the army had returned to Thebes. This was another major step up in his career, for it indicated that he could reach a position of real power in Egypt if he worked well.

Messengers sped back across the border into Egypt to prepare the people for the forthcoming celebrations, and to make sure that the maximum number of men, women, and children would be lining the route to hail the mighty pharaoh's return to the capital.

Nekhebu takes notes while Ramses II discusses the battle with one of his men. In the foreground are some bronze weapons.

Ramses decided that on arrival back in Thebes there would be a special ceremony to award the "Gold of Valor" to those who had most distinguished themselves. Nekhebu felt he had merely done his duty, but the king was pleased with him and so, in front of the whole army, Nekhebu the scribe would be among the few to receive this insignia, to be hung round his neck. At the age of only twenty-five, Nekhebu would be a marked man indeed.

Back on the battlefield, the army was now ready to march. It was formed up just as it had been for the advance to the battle, with an infantry regiment leading the vanguard, immediately followed by trumpeters. There were some gaps in the ranks, but casualties on the Egyptian side had not been heavy.

In front of the pharaoh's chariot walked the most important prisoners, with ropes round their necks, and many with their arms tied behind their backs. Most had their hands trapped in pillories – wooden frames which prevented free movement. It was a most uncomfortable way of undergoing a long march, especially for those who were princes of their own people and unused to hardship.

Once across the border, the rejoicings began. The news had brought first hundreds, then thousands, of people to greet the gallant victors. Priests offered flowers to the pharaoh and his commanders, and songs of victory were sung as shouts rent the air.

By the time the army reached Thebes it seemed that everyone within traveling distance had converged on the capital. Crowds came to watch a number of leading prisoners being executed as an example to any would-be enemies of Egypt. Eight were killed with ceremonial swords, then their bodies were hung from one of the temple walls to impress upon all observers that it was unwise to challenge the might of Egypt.

Next came the selection of gifts of booty for the gods, who would receive the best of what had been captured. The Egyptians believed that it was through the active help of the gods that they had achieved victory over the barbarians. The rest of the loot was to be distributed to the warriors.

Now for the reorganization of the prisoners. Nekhebu had had enough time to plan this work carefully. None was needed for the royal bodyguard, for Ramses had already recruited all he needed from the Shardana, a tall, well-built Mediterranean people who were renowned as pirates before the time when the Egyptians had captured them and hired many of them as soldiers for their army.

So Nekhebu could concentrate on filling the ranks of the rest of the army. Acting as chief scribe, he selected the best of the prisoners with the aid of a general. Both men were directly responsible to the pharaoh himself.

Nekhebu chose carefully, then concentrated on the other part of his task, the selection of men for stone-quarrying and brick-making. He was able to take time off to attend another ceremony, too, in which the army was issued with new weapons and equipment. Again, the pharaoh was present, standing on a dais, as his troops, advancing in single file, picked up weapons from one pile – spears, bows, swords – and equipment, including coats of mail, quivers, and helmets from another. Once again the scribes were present to write everything down. The Egyptians were an efficient race and their scribes claimed to belong to the greatest of all professions because they arranged the destinies of the whole nation.

The prisoners of war await their fate while Nekhebu, in the background, receives his Gold of Valor from Ramses II.

Victory celebrations

On the great day of the triumphal march through Thebes, Nekhebu was allowed to ride in one of the chariots, wearing his Gold of Valor. Few scribes had ever been so honored, and though many maintained that they looked down on the military, there must have been a good number watching who were envious of the young man whose advancement, thanks to the pharaoh, had been so fast.

This was the day when the captured treasures would be laid at the feet of the gods in the temples. In the march many of the prisoners of war, including their leaders, were paraded before the people, then sent to join the rest of the captives, who had already been assigned to their military quarters by Nekhebu and his army colleague. No one thought at this point that it might be unwise to have so large a part of the army – the majority, in fact – made up of foreigners with no reason to feel loyalty for the state which they would be serving; for the moment nothing mattered except the glory of the pharaoh.

The feast held that night in the royal palace was sumptuous. Ramses was seated on a beautifully carved chair, his queen by his side. Nekhebu sat a short distance away, listening to a general who, standing in the center of the room, was giving a vivid account of the victory to those around him. The food and drink, in ornate vessels and jars, was displayed on small tables, and of course, all the guests, regardless of rank, ate with their fingers.

The finest acrobats, dancing girls, and musicians, both Nubian and Egyptian, were there that night to entertain the company. Throughout the night, the sound of music never ceased. We do not know exactly what Egyptian music sounded like, but we know that Egyptian musicians had stringed, woodwind, and brass instruments, in common with orchestras today. They also had drums, clappers, tambourines, and other instruments, and would often clap rhythmically for effect. There were singers, too. It is thought that they may have sounded rather like today's North African singers, or like the exciting flamenco singers of Spain. Like the Spaniards, the Egyptians used a type of castanets.

The air was full of perfume, for several women wore on their heads white cones of solid perfumed wax, which gradually melted, covering the face with an exotic-smelling substance.

For the prisoners, there was no feasting: most were now part of the Egyptian army. A few had been killed and their bodies hanged as an example of what happened to enemies of the great pharaoh.

On the whole, however, Egypt's penal system was not as harsh as might be expected. The worst punishment, for prisoners of war and Egyptian criminals alike, was hard labor in the mines, where living conditions for the prisoners were nightmarish (the nonprisoner miners were treated

While the general describes the recent victory over the Hittites, Nekhebu enjoys the feasting. Ramses, surrounded by servants and musicians, sits on the extreme right.

better, of course). By contrast, stealing was not usually dealt with very harshly in ancient Egypt. Thieves were ordered to return the stolen goods and were fined up to three times their value – by any standards, a merciful treatment. If the victim of the theft were a kindly person, he might excuse the thief from payment. The standard punishment for small crimes was, generally speaking, a good beating.

When the rich people had a legal dispute (perhaps over land or an inheritance), the case would be presided over by no less a person than the vizier, acting as judge. Nekhebu had met the vizier, pharaoh's "prime minister," at the feast to celebrate the victory over the Hittites, and had been most impressed by him. His duties were many. He was pharaoh's deputy, acting for him whenever he was away from the palace in Thebes, minister of war, of irrigation, and of agriculture. He was also responsible for ensuring that not too many trees were felled – a vital job in Egypt, which was extremely short of trees. Sometimes he would accompany Ramses on a campaign instead of remaining in charge at home.

Another person Nekhebu met at the feast was the young, beautiful daughter of one of pharaoh's noblemen. When, soon after, Nekhebu asked for her hand in marriage, her father was delighted to agree to the match and have for a son-in-law this man whom Ramses himself had honored.

Home life

As the years passed, Nekhebu rose to the position of chief adviser to Ramses on architecture and building. His success brought him riches, and two children completed his joy. A casual visitor to his fine villa in Thebes might have found him dressed in a robe of white linen, or even a simple loincloth. (Peasants also wore loincloths, but more often than not they and their families wore nothing.) Nekhebu's wife would probably have been wearing a tight-fitting straight dress held up by shoulder straps. As a woman of rank, she employed dressmakers who excelled in pleating and other artistic effects, and she possessed several splendid cloaks with highly decorated hems.

Like all Egyptians, of both sexes, the couple loved jewelry, and as theirs was a most superstitious race, many of the jewels that they wore had a magical meaning.

Nekhebu wore his hair cropped short, though he put on a fine wig for important occasions, and his wife wore an even more splendid wig over her already elaborately set hair. On top of these wigs they sometimes wore the white wax cones full of perfume, especially for social occasions.

They wore sandals of leather or woven papyrus on their feet, though only on special occasions. Otherwise they went barefoot – as peasants did at all times.

Faces, however, were another matter. Egyptian ladies of fashion must have occasionally kept their husbands waiting before going out, so elaborate was their makeup. They blackened their eyebrows and outlined their eyes in green or black paint, after washing thoroughly all over with a special cleaning paste. (The Egyptians considered washing very important, and tried to wash three times a day.) Makeup boxes were often exquisite as well as useful, and ladies had an astonishing number of toilet implements. They reddened their lips, dyed their fingernails, and enjoyed using subtle perfumes, of which there was a huge range.

Fine furniture and comfortable beds characterized the homes of Nekhebu and his friends. Peasants and desert tribesmen slept on the floor or

34

on the ground, although some well-to-do people slept on reed mats.

Some houses, Nekhebu's among them, had cupboards built into the bedroom walls, and all households, prosperous or not, had one or more chests in which to keep linen or family possessions or both.

Nekhebu's villa had two stories, though many of his friends' homes had only a ground floor. His bedroom had a beautifully painted wall showing a hunting scene, and all his ceilings were painted. There was not much furniture by today's standards.

At mealtimes, servants placed dishes on small tables, for there was no central dining table. Even some of the rich families sat on the floor to eat – just as scribes sat on the ground with their stiff rolls of papyrus propped on their knees to write. Rich and poor alike ate with their fingers.

The Egyptians enjoyed their food. Every sort of bread and cake was made. The favorite fruits were grapes, apples, and pomegranates. Oranges and lemons were not grown in Nekhebu's day. The range of vegetables was enormous. Many were dried for the winter. In fact, the wide range of fruit and vegetables plus the vast amount of meat that they ate must have made the Egyptians' diet an excellent one. Beef and ox were the standard meats, though wild fowl was also popular. Pork was considered unclean. Fish was not eaten everywhere, possibly for religious reasons in some areas: the very unfriendly god Seth may have been the cause of this, for fish were sacred to him.

Wine was Nekhebu's favorite drink. He grew his own grapes and made his wine in a way that would meet the approval of experts today, storing it in jars in his cellar. The vast majority of the people drank beer.

Nekhebu's garden was enchanting. The Egyptians were highly skilled in the art of raising flowers and trees. At one end was a small religious shrine for the use of the family and in the center was a pool. A back gate led out to Nekhebu's estate, dominated by a granary.

He had a number of servants, most of whom lived in a separate building. In charge of them was his chief steward, who, like other senior members of his staff, had small houses to themselves. The biggest room in Nekhebu's house was the living room, with high walls and small windows that let in all the direct light that was needed. Other rooms in the house included a remarkable bathroom, complete with efficient plumbing, and an office, where Nekhebu ran his private empire.

The kitchen was housed in a separate building, which in that hot climate kept smells away from the home. In fact everything was done to make a rich Egyptian family's life as pleasant as possible, and Nekhebu and his wife were lucky to live in an age when they could enjoy to the full a tranquil existence. But then even peasants in Egypt 3000 years ago led happier and more comfortable lives than many millions do today.

Egyptian women loved make-up, and Nekhebu's wife was no exception. She applied kohl to her eyelids with a round-ended rod, and red ochre to her lips with a special brush.

Devotions and death

Long before the ancient Greeks officially "invented" drama, the Egyptians were reveling in it. Their theater was linked closely to religion, with exciting episodes in the lives of their gods providing the stories. Vast crowds of pilgrims came to watch the plays – and even to take part in them! They were given mostly in temples, but sometimes on lakes, and sometimes over a thousand actors would take part in battle scenes.

The gods were treated as familiar human beings, for everyone knew their stories. A great event in the life of Nekhebu and his family was a visit to one such play at Abydos. The plays at Abydos, together with those at Busiris, were the best staged and costumed in Egypt. Nekhebu saw a play that told the story of the god Osiris, a good king who was murdered by the wicked Seth and thrown into the Nile. The combination of professional actors (playing the leading parts), pilgrims

(in the minor roles), and audience shouting and laughing made the whole entertainment a triumph for players and public alike – though, for a religious drama, a very rowdy one. It was all Nekhebu, now a dignified official, could do not to join in with the other spectators.

Although not one Egyptian play has come down to us, enough has survived in descriptions of players, plays, and audiences to show what a notable part the theater occupied in the hearts of the ancient Egyptians. It is further proof that the Egyptians enjoyed life, despite what might be regarded as a morbid concern with death.

Death was by no means a morbid or frightening thought for the Egyptians, but an event to be approached with reason and practicality. For instance, when Nekhebu had reached high rank under the pharaoh, he had selected a site on the bank of the Nile opposite Thebes and, like all important Egyptians, he had spent much time in preparing his final resting place. He had regularly visited the site of his tomb, supervising the build-

The wicked god Seth murders the god Osiris in the passion play attended by Nekhebu at Abydos.

ing of the chamber below ground and the fine building above it, with its courtyard, pool, and a hall of fame decorated with paintings proclaiming important moments in his life.

Much that he would need for the next world was already in place in the tomb, including chairs and beds and even model peasants, made of wood, who would magically do their share of work for their master in the fields of heaven. Arrangements had been made, for which his son would be responsible, for suitable ceremonies to be conducted annually in his memory. And, of course, Nekhebu's mummification had also been arranged in advance. It was carried out during the seventy days after his death, while his family grieved over their great loss.

When, eventually, Nekhebu's last days came, there was great sorrow. An impressive funeral followed, during which the mourners' grief could not be restrained. The women in particular made loud lamentations. They struck their heads, groaning pitifully, smeared their faces with mud, and tore their clothes. Others simply talked of the dead man. At the front of the procession servants carried a large final load of possessions, some of which Nekhebu had been using up to the end. The coffin was drawn by cows and men, and was soon aboard a special boat for its final journey across the Nile. It was towed by a large boat that bore Nekhebu's sorrowing relations.

Many friends and colleagues were there to make the final journey to the tomb, where priests were ready for the ceremony of burial. When the body had been reverently left in its final resting place, the shaft of the tomb was blocked up, and a funeral feast took place in the courtyard above, where musicians sang, accompanying themselves on the harp. All that could have been done for Nekhebu had been done, and his family and friends, for all their sadness, were satisfied that he was doing well in his new state.

On one of the tomb's walls was a long account of Nekhebu's fine character and his services to the state, so that future generations could marvel at his life and great fame in the reign of Ramses II. Naturally, ordinary citizens had no such splendid tombs, and paupers were buried in an ordinary burial pit. But then, the ordinary people in the stable kingdom of ancient Egypt did not expect anything else: each man knew his place, though some, like Nekhebu, managed to rise above it.

Inside Nekhebu's richly decorated tomb, the walls of which tell the story of the great events in his life, an artist works on the decoration of the lid of Nekhebu's coffin.

The afterlife

Every Egyptian was only too well aware of the hard time that awaited him between his death and his arrival – if he was lucky – in the celestial fields. Like every other religion, the Egyptian faith had its own views on what part of the human being survives after death, and by the time of the New Kingdom priests were trying to standardize beliefs that had gradually changed down many centuries.

The ordinary people benefited greatly because, as late as the Old Kingdom, there had been no place for them in heaven. Only the pharaoh and his immediate circle could hope to enjoy an afterlife. Considering the difficulties that were put in the path of the dead, one might think that the ordinary people were lucky simply to enter oblivion, but the old belief was obviously grossly unfair. Only a tiny handful could climb aboard the sun-god Ra's boat and sail to the extreme east of the sky to join the other immortals.

After the all-powerful kings of the Old Kingdom had passed into history, a combination of more human pharaohs and the worship of the democratic and progressive god Osiris gave every Egyptian the chance to reach paradise.

To complicate matters, the Egyptians divided the soul into several parts, or, rather, clearly recognized several sorts of soul. The most important is for us the most mysterious. It was called the *Ka* and seems to have been the main soul, born when a man was born and returning to him at the time of his death. It then lived on in a mummy, eating offerings from relatives and priests. Meanwhile the *Ba* soul, usually portrayed as a human-headed bird, came from the body at death to roam in any form it chose. The *Ba* was perhaps the nearest to our modern idea of a spiritual soul, the *Ka* being a source of energy or life-force or physical vitality.

Then there was the *Akh* that made the long journey to heaven, while the mysterious *Sekhem* was somewhat similar to the *Ka*.

It will be seen from all this why the Egyptians filled the tombs with so many useful things. Not only the *Ka* needed attention in the tomb, but the *Akh* also needed every sort of item from books to furniture just as much as the *Ka* did. For this reason the tomb of an important person, such as Nekhebu, would contain stone or wooden figures to work for him when he was asked to do his share of hard labor in the fields of heaven.

However, not everyone reached the fields of heaven. As everyone knew, the journey was hazardous in the extreme. Aboard his ship of death, the dead person would set out on the dark Nile that the Egyptians believed flowed beneath their own beloved river. He had successfully

An Egyptian mourning scene: a widow kneels and caresses the feet of her dead husband's mummy during the funerary rites of a member of the nobility.

Judgement scene from The Book of the Dead, *showing the weighing of the heart. Anubis adjusts the balance, while Thoth records the result.*

crossed the mountains of death, but now he was approaching a nightmare region where monsters dwelled. If he was a coward, he was doomed at the start, for the fiends would capture him and torture him, then burn him or eat him alive.

The hazards included a boiling lake and a lake of fire, a terrible serpent called Apaphis, and a snake that spat poison. When the long journey was over, there was an even stiffer test in the hall of Maat, the goddess of truth.

She would put the traveler's heart in one of the twin pans of her scales and in the other her emblem, a magical feather. In some versions of the trial, the feather would be replaced by an image of Maat herself (see above). This test made even the monsters seem puny by comparison. The evidence of the scales would decide whether the traveler was destined to enter paradise or be doomed to a horrific fate.

Anubis, the dog-headed god, would come forward to adjust the balance, while Thoth, who had the head of an ibis, a large wading bird, acting as a heavenly scribe, would enter the result of the balancing on papyrus. The scene was made even more impressive – or horrifying, depending on the character of the would-be entrant to heaven – by the presence of forty-two assessors, who were there to act as a jury. The number was carefully chosen, for there was one assessor for every sin that could lose the dead person a place in paradise.

So the trial would begin, with the impassive assessors gazing at the newcomer.

Happy the applicant whose heart balanced the magical feather, for this meant that he had succeeded. Forward stepped the god Horus to lead him to Osiris, who was waiting for him in his shrine. Soon he would be on his way to heavenly fields where he would once again meet his family and friends, who had already made the great journey. One of their favorite occupations, as he would soon discover, was sailing on the heavenly Nile. In other words, the Egyptians' idea of paradise was like an even more pleasant version of their own beloved homeland.

But what about the applicant who was weighed in the balance and found wanting?

A really dreadful fate awaited him, for if his heart was found to be heavier than the feather, that meant his sins outweighed his virtues. In such cases the Devourer would at once appear, a ghastly-looking creature with the head of a crocodile, a lion's forequarters, and the rear of a hippopotamus. This appalling apparition would promptly devour the flesh and bones and drink the blood of the miserable wretch. Human nature being what it is, such an initiation ceremony would not seem to hold out much hope for the majority. But the Egyptians were optimists.

39

III After the pharaohs
The decline of ancient Egypt

Alexander the Great

No empire has lasted as long as ancient Egypt's, and, as we have seen, for most of that time the people, even the humblest, seem to have been reasonably happy. Yet soon after the reign of Ramses II, around 1100 B.C., Egypt's decline started. Its prosperity became almost too great for its own good. Many foreign slaves were imported, the army was filled with hired foreign troops instead of patriotic Egyptians, government officials became slack, foreigners began to settle in Egypt in growing numbers, and the peasants became less contented.

The descendants of Ramses II and III were weaklings, or so it seems from the little evidence we have, and they lost control to the rebellious priests. These rulers were idle and unwarlike and used too many foreign troops to fight for them. Slowly, the once glorious state of Egypt slumped into ill rule and its reputation sank. Eventually, the kingdom was split into small states, which made it easy for the Ethiopians to take over the land.

A much worse misfortune was to befall Egypt. About 670 B.C. the terrible Assyrians invaded, capturing Thebes and sacking the city – a blood-drenched event that sent a shudder of fear through every nation that was within striking distance of Assyria. Once more Egyptians were divided up into small principalities, which in the past had always spelled unhappiness. Occasionally a strong ruler would appear who gave a generation a taste of what its ancestors had enjoyed in the old days, but usually there was fear, anxiety, and unhappiness.

Then came the Persians, eager to seize the rich Nile Valley. A Persian king named Cambyses stormed Memphis and became the ruler of Egypt. He was followed by the great Persian ruler Darius, who provided the conquered nation with an excellent government and built up its trade, not least by finishing a canal from the Nile to the Red Sea.

The old royal line of Egypt did its best to quell rebellions and sometimes drove the invaders back for a while, but, finally, the last native king of Egypt fled to Ethiopia and the Persians systematically ruined a once proud nation. So hated were they that when the brilliant Greek general Alexander the Great defeated them and took over their empire, the Egyptians welcomed him as if he were one of their own.

It was in 332 B.C. that Alexander conquered the Persian Empire, and in the short time that he stayed in Egypt, he proceeded to bring the country back to life. He founded the fine city that bears his name, Alexandria, he respected the Egyptian religion and even worshipped the local gods, and he brought peace.

But Alexander, one of the greatest conquerors in history, who led his armies as far east as India, died young, and his generals divided up his kingdom. The general in charge of Egypt was named Ptolemy, and the Ptolemies were to rule the country from 323 to 30 B.C.

The first Ptolemy was a determined man. On the principle that possession of Alexander's dead body would act as a good luck charm and keep the country safe from yet more invasions, he decided to obtain it for himself. It had been arranged for the dead hero to be buried in neutral territory at an oasis called Amon, but Ptolemy's men met the funeral procession and simply took control.

Soter, the first of the Ptolemies

Having gotten the body, he proceeded to take it to Alexandria, where it was buried with the utmost pomp. No one was prepared to argue with Ptolemy's formidable army.

He and his successors were determined to make the city not just the greatest in the eastern Mediterranean, but also the cultural and intellectual capital. Ptolemy II started a library and museum which both became so famous that men of learning from all over the ancient world flocked to Alexandria. The city itself was a breathtaking sight. Scientists and scholars thrived in its atmos-

phere, and soon the famous library had a million books – centuries before the invention of printing. Meanwhile the sensible Ptolemies, careful to keep the peace with the still influential priests, restored many of the temples to something approaching their former glory.

Alas, once again time weakened the character of the ruling dynasty of Egypt. Once the name of Ptolemy had stood for authority, wisdom, and might, but later Ptolemies decided that a luxurious life beside the Nile was pleasanter than hard administrative work. And by now the most remarkable, if not the most attractive, of all the peoples of the ancient world were on their triumphant march to world domination: the Romans.

It came about that the last of the Ptolemies, and one of the greatest, was in no position to save her royal line. This was Cleopatra (69–30 B.C.), one of the most famous women who ever lived. She was co-ruler of Egypt with her younger brother, but was ousted by his guardians. It was the great Roman Julius Caesar who, after falling in love with her, restored her to her throne.

Cleopatra was of pure Greek descent, like all the Ptolemies, and was very beautiful – so beautiful that she immediately ensnared the Roman general Antony when he met her. Their love story – the subject of several plays, including Shakespeare's *Antony and Cleopatra*, and a succession of motion pictures – changed history. Because of Cleopatra, Antony fought a civil war with the supporters of Julius Caesar's successor, Octavius, and risked a major sea battle at Actium. She fled with her ships and he followed her, giving up half the Roman world for love.

Tragically, Antony heard that she had killed herself, and, no longer wishing to live, he fell upon his sword. Then, hearing that she was still alive, he had himself carried to her. Their reunion was brief, and he died in her arms.

Cleopatra could not affect the cold-hearted Octavius as she had the warm-blooded Antony, and, rather than appear as a prisoner at his triumph in Rome, she killed herself.

So Octavius, soon to be the Emperor Augustus Caesar, took over the ancient kingdom of Egypt and turned it into a vast private estate for the rulers of Rome. Its people's taxes helped provide a huge income for the emperors of Rome. From having been the most powerful nation on earth, Egypt had become a political backwater. The glorious 3000-year saga was finally over.

Elizabeth Taylor and Richard Burton star as Cleopatra and Mark Antony in the motion picture Cleopatra *(©1963, Twentieth Century-Fox Productions, Ltd. All rights reserved.)*

Dead kings, living stone

Napoleon Bonaparte in Egypt

No one who has read this far will surely be in any doubt that ancient Egypt's civilization was a great one. Yet for well over a thousand years, indeed until the nineteenth century, that greatness was virtually forgotten. The Greeks and Romans had little interest in Egypt – with a few notable exceptions such as Alexander the Great – except as a place to be ruled and exploited. But the Romans ruled well and citizens could go anywhere safely.

Then came the great silence. The Christians, so cruelly treated by the Romans, began to exert their influence. By the fourth century A.D. they were in power, and were not interested in preserving Egypt's pagan religion or its monuments. Soon no one understood the key to Egyptian civilization, the hieroglyphs, not even the Egyptians themselves. The next conquerors, the Arabs, did not concern themselves with the past, and Europe was only just emerging from the barbarism that followed the fall of the Roman Empire. No one visited Egypt except for a few bold pilgrims on their way to the Holy Land, who went to Egypt because it had a great many biblical associations.

Those who visited it saw the remains of past glory in a far finer state than they are today. Theories on the pyramids varied from a belief that they had been built by witchcraft to one more widely held that they had been built as granaries.

In the late Middle Ages, when the glories of ancient Greece and Rome and their cultures were being rediscovered, no one thought of Egypt as worth more than an occasional glance. Those who visited it lapped up foolish legends about it. By the seventeenth century few visitors were venturing south of Cairo, the pyramids, and the sphinx. No one knew where Thebes was, though its fame had been revived when men of learning rediscovered the ancient Greeks, and read about the fabulous city in the works of the celebrated poet Homer. Yet visitors had been to Thebes without realizing it: they were hoping to find it "hundred-gated" as Homer had claimed it was. At last scholarly visitors began to study the strange remains in Egypt at least a little scientifically. One of them, a Jesuit named Father Claude Sicard, who traveled in Egypt between 1707 and 1726, not only found the lost city of Thebes, but realized what he had found. He saw no less than four city gates almost intact and traced the streets. By 1722, when he had been as far up the Nile as Aswan, he had identified twenty-four complete temples in Egypt and other marvels, though his finds were known to few.

Soon the rush – a modest enough one at first – began, but though realization of Egypt's former glory started to grow, most of the scholars and travelers did vast amounts of damage as they grabbed what they could by methods fair and foul, including gunpowder. Strangely, most of them thought that the mysterious hieroglyphics were mystic symbols, not a form of writing.

The real turning point came when the French invaded Egypt in 1798 under Napoleon Bonaparte. The military action was no great success, but much to the credit of France, engineers, scholars, and artists accompanied the battalions and eventually unearthed the Rosetta Stone.

As learning increased so did the number of people ruthlessly seeking remnants. Belzoni, whom we have already met, may be forgiven for his methods, because he was one of the first great archaeologists, though a primitive one. Others merely butchered the past. Despite the fact that the Egyptians were beginning to realize something of the glories of their ancestors, they allowed many old buildings to be destroyed so that the ground could be used for quarries.

Above: the temple of Queen Hatshepsut in Thebes.

Below: Giovanni Belzoni and his most famous feat – transporting the colossal bust of Ramses II to the Nile (see page 16).

By the 1860s, the situation had improved mainly because of a remarkable Frenchman named Mariette. Almost single-handedly he forced Egypt to protect, not destroy, the past and to ensure that her greatest treasures remained in their homeland. Thanks to his example the Cairo Museum, rather than the Louvre in Paris or the British Museum, is the world's greatest treasury of ancient Egyptian culture. After Mariette came the first great modern archaeologist, Flinders Petrie, at which point we are almost back where we began – at the moment when Howard Carter saw those "wonderful things."

The rescue of Abu Simbel

In the last resort people are more important than any monument. But some monuments are so stupendous that they have inspired tremendous human efforts to preserve them.

This is exactly what happened to the colossal statues of Ramses II at Abu Simbel. These were threatened by a 297.6 mile (480 kilometers) long lake, which was being created by the construction of the great Aswan Dam. The thought of the statues being submerged forever beneath the waters of the Nile was unbearable for many thousands of people despite the fact that most of them had never had the opportunity to visit them. More than fifty countries contributed to a fund to save the monuments, the largest amounts being from the U.S. and Egypt itself. Engineers from West Germany, Egypt, France, Italy, and Sweden formed a team to tackle "Operation Abu Simbel."

First the mountainside that housed the statues and temples was cut open to clear an area round the monuments, and the temples behind them. Five hundred thousand tons of rock had to be removed from above the temples before workmen could begin the process of cutting each monument into sections. The blocks were stored for a time up the hillside. The heaviest of the one thousand or so blocks was thirty tons.

The temples and statues were reassembled 206.7 feet (63 meters) above the original site, the blocks – which were hardly damaged at all – being injected with plastic cement at their joints. The result was a complete reconstruction of the monuments made safe for the foreseeable future.

This unique operation cost about $135 million (£45 million) and took only five years to complete.

Originally it had been hoped to lift the monuments in their entirety by using an extraordinary jacking process, but this Italian idea, inspired as it was, had to be abandoned because of lack of money.

The work force was a veritable United Nations. There were more than a thousand laborers, engineers, technicians, and archaeologists on the site when the undertaking was at its climax in the late 1960s. Among the languages heard hanging on the clear Egyptian air were Arabic, Italian, German, Swedish, French, and English. And almost as soon as Abu Simbel was saved, the fight began to save the Greco-Roman temples at Philae, flooded for nine months of every year since the erection of the old Aswan Dam in 1902.

These major tasks are but a fraction of what has been and is happening elsewhere in Egypt. Some ten thousand sites are being worked and finds are continuous. The dry climate and the Egyptian sand has ensured that most of them are in extraordinarily good condition. The incredible fact is that nothing – paint, gold, papyrus, cloth – seems to decay. However, in some places there is a race against time because the Aswan Dam has increased the amount of irrigation and so raised the level of underground water. This in turn causes and will cause a growing number of buildings to collapse.

Interior of one of the temples at Abu Simbel, saved for posterity by a worldwide campaign.

So the fight is on, and it is a fight that is being won. The Egyptians, having learned from European experts, are now highly trained excavators themselves, with the added incentives of patriotism and the expanding tourist trade to spur them on to greater effort. In one three-year period a thousand objects were found at Karnak, and there is no prospect of a slowing down in the discovery rate unless the workers are forced to stop for a war.

The truth is that the story of ancient Egypt is

Façade of the temple of Ramses II. The entrance is flanked by seated colossi of the king, nearly 70 feet high. In the center is a statue of Re-Horakhy, falcon-headed god of the horizon, and along the cornice sits a row of baboons, sacred to Thoth, god of wisdom.

only just beginning. The giant archaeological and historical jigsaw puzzle is gradually taking shape, but it will be many years before all the facts, or even the major part of them, relating to the world's first great civilization are revealed.

The Ramseum.